Over 100 Drills And Conditioning Exercises

Advertising Works, 32 Algerine St, Berkley, MA 02779
2004

Over 100 Drills And Conditioning Exercises

Collected and Presented by
Karen M. Goeller

Drills and Conditioning Exercises

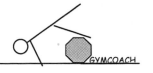

(Feedback mostly from 2nd edition of drills book.)

"...FANTASTIC! ... a goldmine for new team & pre-team coaches...high quality, useful, and reasonably priced..."
SJ Clifford, GTC, NY (Nat'l TOPS Testing Host)

"SUPER book, filled with drills! Sellers polite..."
M. Maxwell, RI

"Super book, recommending to all my friends, fast delivery, helpful exercises!"
N Stevens-Brown, CA (American Vaulting Assoc. Coach)

"Great book! My daughter loves it. A#1 seller. Would recommend to all!!!!"
D. Conine, OH

"It is a sum up of success on gymnastics...Let the words of New Generation exist with the day in this book"
Meng Kui Wang 40+ yrs in gymnastics, Men's Judge, Author, Nat'l Recruiter for China

*"I received the book today and I am extremely pleased.
Thanks so much for a great deal. "*
L Robbins, VA

"The explanations were clear and the pictures helped."
M Soto, NY

"Your writing on gymnastics education is very good."
P Spadaro, NY USAG Chairman & VP USAIGC

"I bring mine to the gym everyday!"
C Brouns, MA YMCA

"The exercises look great" (Sells book at camp store.)
M Jacobsen, Owner USGTC

"Well written, easy to read, good conditioning ideas. Thanks!"
J Wisley, WA

"Great product!! My daughter loves it!!"
M Mackins, NY

"Thanks for the book, its perfect.."
J. Latshaw, NJ

"I received the book and laminates and am pleased with them! After looking through it, I realized that most of these were drills that we were taught in our coaching class at Indiana University, but have forgotten over the years. Good job putting that all together! Thanks."
D Russell

www.GymnasticsDrills.com

Over 100 Drills and Conditioning Exercises

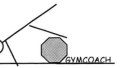

This book includes drills and strength exercises that have been used with Karen's athletes for many years.

Although the drills, when done correctly have proven challenging to gymnasts of all levels, they are most useful to the developing gymnasts in levels one through eight.

Positive feedback has come from many people, including the coaches at a YMCA who used the original handwritten version, the USAG NYS Chairman, and the owner of the gymnastics camp USGTC!

As the owner of a gymnastics training facility for nearly ten years and a gymnastics coach for well over 20 yers, Karen has spent thousands of hours coaching, teaching skills through progressions, drills, strength, and flexibility.

Her gym has employed a sports-scientist and many elite coaches simultaneously, including the National Recruiter for all sports in China, Meng Kui Wang, Former Broadway Dancer, Renville Duncan, and the 1996 USATT National Champion, Tony Flores. Karen has been fortunate enough to work with these coaches for several years and learn a great deal from them.

She considers it a privilege to have worked at Karolyi's Gymnastics Camp in Texas for seven summers as well as at US Gymnastics Training Camp held in Massachusetts and International Gymnastics Camp in Pennsylvania for ten years of Holiday Clinics. Working at these camps along with working for Paul Spadaro and attending many USA Gymnastics events such as Regional Congress and the National TOPS Training Camp have all been contributing factors to her vast knowledge of the sport. Karen has great gratitude for all those who were so generous with their knowledge!

www.GymnasticsDrills.com

Table of Contents

RUNNING DRILLS FOR VAULT AND TUMBLING 1

Arm Motion \ Arm Swing

1. Have your athlete kneel or stand.
2. Have your athlete lift one arm to a forward middle position. Their elbow should be the same height as their shoulder.
3. Next have them bend that arm so that their fingers are pointing toward the ceiling. The bend should be 90 degrees.
4. Once they have the first arm position correct, have them lift the opposite arm behind them so that their elbow is as close to shoulder height as possible. Once that arm is lifted, have them bend it to a 90 degree angle as well. Their fingers may be at hip height.
5. Once they can form those shapes with their arms, have them swing\switch their arms so that the opposite arm is in front.
6. Have your athlete continue the arm motion for the run until they can perform it rapidly.

They will need this arm swing for their run.

Lunge Walks & Exploding Lunges

1. Take a large step with right foot.
2. Keeping left foot behind, place left knee on floor, keeping chest upright.
3. Left arm swings forward; left elbow should be almost even with shoulder and bent at a 90 degree angle.
4. Right arm swings back; right elbow as high as possible and bent at a 90 degree angle.
5. Stand and simultaneously repeat steps 1-4 with opposite leg and arm.
6. Athlete should stand up as tall as possible while stepping forward to next low lunge.
7. **Once mastered**, have your athlete perform an **explosive jump** from their knees and switch legs in the air between every few Lunge Walks. Have them land back in the low lunge (knees at 90 degree angle) kneeling position.

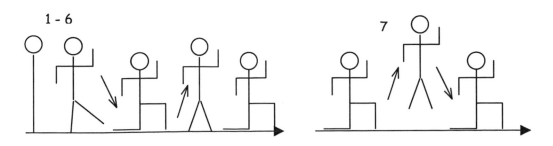

Notes

RUNNING DRILLS FOR VAULT AND TUMBLING 2

Knee Lift (High Knees)

1. With a Marching Motion **step forward with the right leg and then immediately lift the left knee to hip height and the left foot to the height of the right knee.**
2. **Simultaneously lift the right arm forward so that the elbow is shoulder height and the fingers are facing the ceiling. The left elbow should be lifted up and back. Both arms should remain bent with a 90 degree angle and swing alternately throughout the exercise.**
3. Once the Marching Knee Lift is mastered, perform the exercise with a **Running Motion.**
4. Swing left arm back, keeping the elbow bent and 90 degrees; using a running motion
5. Swing legs and arms rapidly, but travel forward slowly in order to focus on the actual knee lift with each step.

Kick Butt

1. With a **Walking Motion** step forward with the right leg and then immediately lift left heel up to touch buttocks.
2. Simultaneously lift the left arm forward so that the elbow is shoulder height and the fingers are facing the ceiling. The right elbow should be lifted up and back. Both arms should remain bent with a 90 degree angle and swing alternately throughout the exercise.
3. Simultaneously switch legs and arms, kicking buttocks with right heel and swinging right arm forward.
4. Once the Walking Butt Kick is mastered, perform the exercise with a **Running Motion.**
5. Swing legs and arms rapidly, but travel forward slowly in order to focus on the actual heel lift with each step.

Notes

RUNNING DRILLS FOR VAULT AND TUMBLING 3

Power Skips (Skipping with Explosive Movements for Height)

1. Step with left leg, immediately and aggressively bring right knee up and right toe next to the left knee.
2. As the knee and toe are being lifted, perform a hop with the supporting leg.
3. Just as aggressively, Lift the left arm up and forward to initiate the arm swing, using the opposite arms as the legs.
4. In between each power skip, take two steps in order to focus on one leg at a time.
5. Have your athletes try this exercise backwards. Be careful not to let them trip over anything or bump into anything.

One Legged Lifts and Skips

1. With a Marching Motion step forward with the right leg and then immediately lift the left knee to hip height and the left foot to the height of the right knee. At the top of the lift, rise up on the toes\ball of supporting foot.
2. Simultaneously lift the right arm forward so that the elbow is shoulder height and the fingers are facing the ceiling.
3. The left elbow should be lifted up and back. Both arms should remain bent with a 90 degree angle and swing alternately throughout the exercise.
4. Once the knee lift is at it's highest point, return the foot to the floor (step forward onto that foot) and take another step forward in order to repeat the knee lift using the same knee down the entire runway .
5. Once one side\leg is learned, perform the exercise using the other side\leg the next time.
6. Once the one Legged Lift is mastered, perform the exercise with a **Hopping\Skipping Motion** on the supporting leg and swing the arms as if running.
7. Swing legs and arms rapidly and explosively for the skips.

1-5 ... Walks

6 - 7 ... Skips

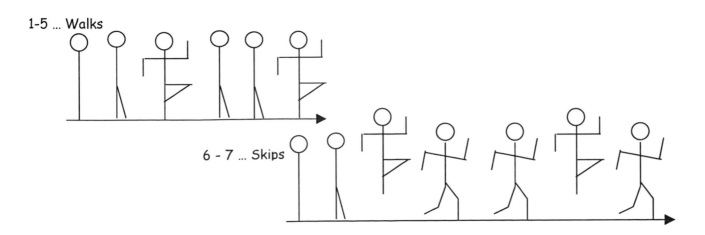

Notes

RUNNING DRILLS FOR VAULT AND TUMBLING 4

Deer Runs

1. Step with leaping motion onto right leg. Swing left arm forward, keeping it bent throughout exercise.
2. Immediately kick left leg back and up, higher than buttocks while traveling forward.
3. Immediately leap\bounce to left leg bringing left knee to forward/high position.
4. Simultaneously kick rear\right leg in a stretched position up and back.
5. Continue leaping from leg to leg lifting the front knee high and back leg high.
6. Both arms should remain bent with a 90 degree angle and swing alternately throughout the exercise.

Accelerations

1. Perform the knee lift\high knees drill in place.
2. Start movement\run forward slowly for the first 4-6 steps.
3. Suddenly increase speed (accelerate to top speed) as quickly as possible.
4. Both arms should remain bent with a 90 degree angle and swing alternately throughout the exercise.
5. Arm speed should increase with leg speed.

Quick Feet

1. Perform the knee lift\high knees drill in place, but move feet\legs as rapidly as possible.
2. After the sixth or seventh step quickly initiate a sprint forward.
3. Accelerate to top speed as quickly as possible.
4. Both arms should remain bent with a 90 degree angle and swing alternately throughout the exercise.
5. The difference between this and the acceleration is that this drill calls for rapid movement from the start and the acceleration allows the athlete to pick up speed gradually.

Notes

RUNNING DRILLS FOR VAULT AND TUMBLING 5

Sprints

1. Run at top speed down runway past horse or other marker appropriate for sport. For gymnastics, the diagonal of floor exercise is highly recommended for higher safety regarding shock absorption.
2. Run at top speed over spring board as if it is not there.
3. Run at top speed into hurdle round off or to a jump on the spring board.
4. Run down hill in order to increase speed of muscles during running motion.
5. Both arms should remain bent with a 90 degree angle and swing alternately throughout the exercise.
6. Arm speed should increase with leg speed.

Sprints

1. Place spring board or other marker appropriate for sport on running surface (runway or floor exercise).
2. For gymnastics, I recommend the diagonal of floor exercise for higher safety regarding shock absorption.
3. Run at top speed down runway and over marker\spring board (as if it is not there) and continue at that speed for an appropriate distance.

Once the athlete is comfortable running over marker\board at top speed you can vary the skills to be performed from the sprint.

For Gymnastics:

1. Run at top speed into hurdle and cartwheel or a round off if not using the board.
2. It the athlete is running over the board, have them perform a straight jump on the spring board and land on an appropriate mat.

Both arms should remain bent with a 90 degree angle and swing alternately throughout the exercise.
Arm speed should increase with leg speed.

Notes

RUNNING DRILLS FOR VAULT AND TUMBLING 6

Hill Runs

1. Start at edge of runway \mat stack.
2. Sprint down the hill and continue at top speed the entire length of the runway or the remainder of the floor exercise diagonal.
3. Both arms should remain bent with a 90 degree angle and swing alternately throughout the exercise.
4. Arm speed should increase with leg speed.

The muscles will become more accustomed to reacting quicker, producing faster runs\sprints.

Hill Runs Over Object (Past Marker)

1. **Place a springboard** about 10-15 feet away from hill.
2. Perform **same sprint** as above, running at top speed downhill and continue running over and past the spring board as if it is not there.
3. Continue running at top speed until end of runway or floor.

For Gymnastics:
1. Run at top speed down hill and straight jump on board, using correct arm technique and body position in air.
2. Place appropriate mat in landing area.

Notes

VAULTING DRILLS 1

Three Board Hurdle

This is an underarm swing/hurdle drill.

1. Line up 3 boards, making sure they are very close\touching each other.
2. Place an appropriate landing mat at end.
3. Have the athletes jump from board one, to two, to three quickly and then land and stick on the mat.
4. Make sure the arm swing is used, the buttocks is under, the chest is up, and the body is tight.
5. Make sure the arms move quickly from side-low position, forward-middle, to a forward-high position; using arms to lift body.

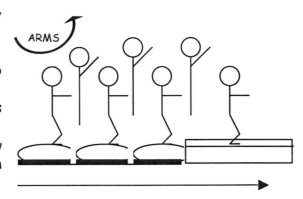

Handstand Hop\Block

1. Place board in front of a low mat stack or landing mat.
2. Have your gymnast kick to handstand on board.
3. Tell them to immediately hop up to folded panel mats using a quick shrug motion\block of the shoulders.
4. The more experienced gymnasts can also do this drill from a low mat to the board for better shock absorption.

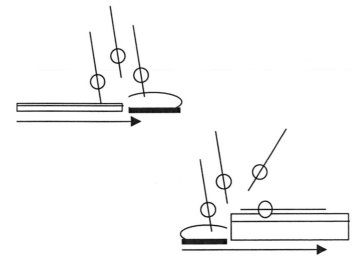

Handstand Hop\Block and Fall

1. Place board in front of a very soft landing mat.
2. Have your gymnast kick to handstand on board.
3. Tell them to immediately block\pop up to fall onto back on very soft and slightly raised mat.
4. Make sure your gymnasts are very tight.

Handstand, Hop, Hop, and Fall

1. Have your gymnast kick to handstand or near handstand on spring board.
2. Remind your gymnast to keep their stomach tight in order to prevent injury.
3. Tell them to immediately block/pop up to a handstand on raised mat or wedge mat.
4. Immediately after the very brief handstand on raised mat, tell them to block/pop up to fall onto back on very soft and slightly raised mat.

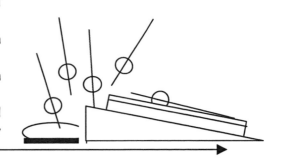

Notes

VAULTING DRILLS 2

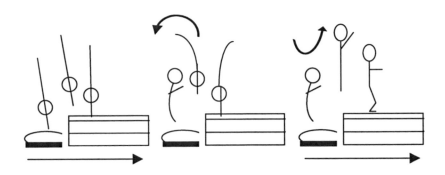

Snap Down to Bounce Up

1. Place a mat stack the long way (as if an extension of the board) in front of a spring board.
2. Have your gymnast kick to handstand on mats.
3. Have them snap down\get their chest up to land on feet on the board.
4. As soon as their feet land on the board, have them arm-circle forward and up to straight jump up to the mat stack.

Once this is mastered:

1. Your gymnast can kick to a handstand on the board.
2. Then have them to immediately hop up to the mats (in handstand position).
3. Next have them snap down\get their chest up to land on feet on the board.
4. As soon as their feet land on the board, have them arm circle forward and up to straight jump up to the mat stack.

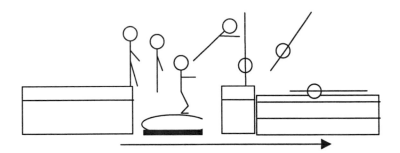

Drop and Pop

1. Place a spring board between two spotting blocks or mat stacks a spring board.
2. Then place a longer mat stack with a very soft landing area at the end.
3. Have your gymnast stand on spotting block.
4. Then have them step down\jump to board.
5. They must then immediately hurdle, using the arm swing upward, and jump to handstand on mat stack.
6. Once in the hand stand, they must push\block\pop up to land on back on the very soft mat or portable pit on their back.

Notes

VAULTING DRILLS 3

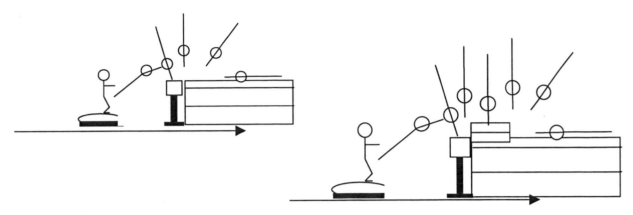

Handspring Pop\Block to Back

1. Set up a high mat stack behind the vault table or use the stack without the table for the less experienced gymnasts.
2. Have your gymnast run at top speed\sprint toward the board and table.
3. As they approach he board instruct them to jump on spring board.
4. Once they hit the spring board and jump up, have them perform a handspring vault.
5. They must land on their back on a pit or soft stack of mats

Handspring, Block, Block
1. The next drill is performed the same as above, but raise height of mats higher than the table.
2. Rather than immediately landing on their back, have your gymnast block\pop up to a handstand on mat that is higher than the table band then block\pop to land on their back on the soft mat.

Handspring to Feet on Stack
1. After this drill is mastered, allow your gymnast to handspring to feet on mat stack.

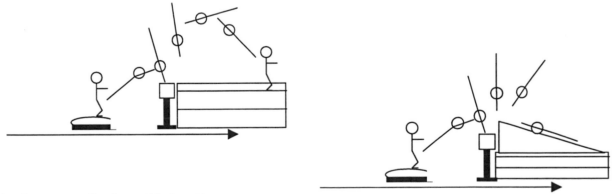

Handspring to Back on Wedge Mat

1. Set up a mat stack, but place a wedge mat on top.
2. Once they hit the spring board and jump up, have them perform a handspring vault.
3. They must land on their back on the soft wedge\stack of mats.

This should feel more like the landing position while continuing to work on body tightness.

VAULTING DRILLS 4

Half-On and Miss Feet

1. Have your gymnast perform a Half-On Vault.
2. They must run at top speed\sprint toward the spring board and table.
3. As they approach he board instruct them to jump on spring board.
4. Once they contact the spring board and jump up, have them half turn/twist before hands contact the table.
5. They must block\pop up and lift chest immediately by pushing down on table.
6. They should feel and look like they are standing in the air, facing the table.
7. The gymnast must continue to rise and then fall to their back on a very soft wedge mat, missing their feet and remaining tight.

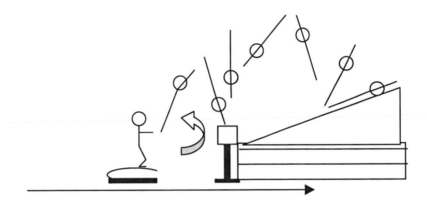

Notes

CONDITIONING AND DRILLS FOR BARS 1

Pull Ups & V Pull Ups

1. Have your gymnast hang from a bar with a straight body or with toes at bar height for the "V".
2. For the "V" Pull Up, the toes must face the ceiling throughout pull up and legs remain close to bar throughout the exercise. (keep V shape).
3. Keeping hands slightly wider than shoulder width, pull collar bones to bar and elbows to ribs.
4. Perform this exercise with palms facing in, using a narrower than shoulder grip and also with a mixed grip to strengthen a variety of areas.
5. The rings may also be used for pull ups.

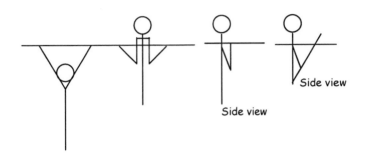

Short Pull Ups ("V" Position)

1. Have your gymnast sit on floor in straddle.
2. Next have them reach up on rope as high as possible while keeping buttocks and legs on floor.
3. Once they have gripped the rope, instruct them to pull their elbows toward their ribs, lifting their entire body as a unit off floor, holding straddle L position.

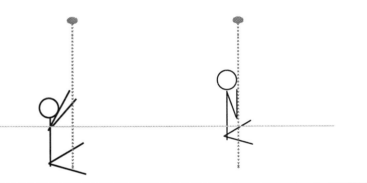

Short Pull Ups (Pike Position)

1. Have your gymnast sit under the beam in a pike position.
2. Next have them grasp the top of beam.
3. Then instruct them to pull their elbows towards their ribs, lifting the body as one unit.
4. Make sure they keep the L position throughout the pull up and the lowering portion of the exercise.

Notes

CONDITIONING AND DRILLS FOR BARS 2

Bent Arm Levers

1. Have your gymnast hang from a bar. Be ready to spot them.
2. Instruct your gymnast to perform a pull up.
3. Next instruct your gymnast to lean back, straighten elbows, and simultaneously pull thighs to the bar. Their body must move as one tight, hollow unit.
4. Once your gymnast is hanging upside down with straight arms and their thighs on the bar, instruct them to pull their chin back over bar and lower legs to return to top of a pull up position.

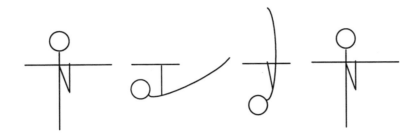

Straight Arm Levers

1. Have your gymnast hang from a bar.
2. Be ready to spot them.
3. Keeping their arms straight, instruct them to lift their toes towards the ceiling and their thighs towards bar.
4. Once upside down with their thighs on the bar, allow them to slowly lower their body to a straight hang position.

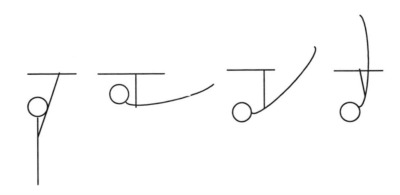

Notes

CONDITIONING AND DRILLS FOR BARS 3

Hollow Toes to Thighs

1. Have your gymnast hang from a bar. Be ready to spot them.
2. Next have them lift their ankles to the bar. ("Leg Lift")
3. Keeping their arms straight, instruct them to slide their legs up bar until their thighs are on bar and they are hanging upside down in a similar position to the top of the straight arm lever.
4. Next instruct them to slowly lower their legs, but keep their ankles on the bar.
5. Have them repeat several before stopping.

This drill is useful for glide kips and clear hip circles.

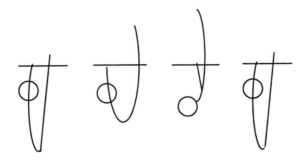

Modified Candlestick Pulls

1. Have your gymnast lie on their back holding the bar base or something very stable that ill not fall on them.
2. Keeping their arms straight and hips open/straight have them pull up to a candlestick position.
3. Once at the top of the modified candlestick, their toes should be pointed outward and upward, not straight up, as in the traditional candlestick position.
4. Instruct your gymnast to slowly lower their legs back to the starting position, lying flat on the floor..
5. Be sure their entire body lifts and lowers as one unit.

Notes

CONDITIONING AND DRILLS FOR BARS 4

Leg Lifts for Glide Kips

1. Place a block or mat stack beneath the low bar.
2. Have your gymnast lie on their back on the block, holding bar as if just completed a glide.
3. Make sure they keep their arms straight, arms near their ears, their shoulders and hips open, and their legs straight.
4. Instruct them to keep their head off the block and between their ears.
5. Instruct them to quickly lift their toes\ankles towards bar.
6. Next have them slowly lower their legs back to the extended glide position and again quickly lift their legs, performing several repetitions.

Glides

1. Have your gymnast stand slightly further than arms distance from low bar.
2. Instruct them to jump, immediately lift toes forward and tuck buttocks under while in air.
3. Once in air, they must grasp the bar, holding a hollow and slightly piked position.
4. They must then swing\glide forward, keeping their feet off the mat and reaching an extended position.
5. Either allow them to swing backward and connect as many glides as possible.
6. Or allow them to release the bar while extended to land on their feet on a mat on the opposite side of bar. Be ready to spot them for this one.

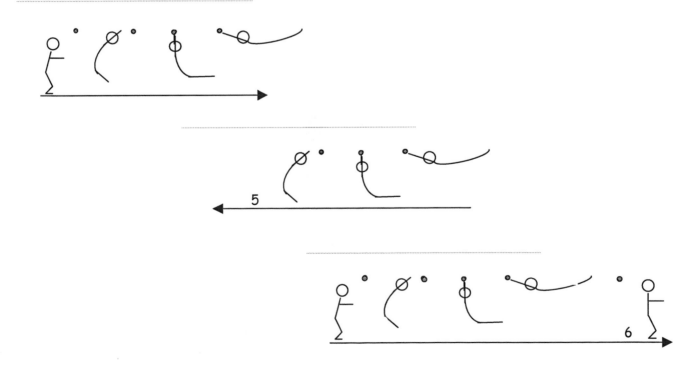

Collected and Presented by Karen M. Goeller Copyright © 2001

Notes

CONDITIONING AND DRILLS FOR BARS 5

Glide and Toes to Bar

1. Have your gymnast stand slightly further than arms distance from low bar.
2. Instruct them to jump, immediately lift toes forward and tuck buttocks under while in air.
3. They must immediately grasp bar, holding a hollow and slightly piked position.
4. Once on the bar, your gymnast must swing\glide forward, keeping their feet off the mat and reaching an extended position.
5. Once they are extended, instruct them to bring their toes\ankles to bar and hold them on the bar, even when the body swings\falls (due to gravity) to the hanging position.

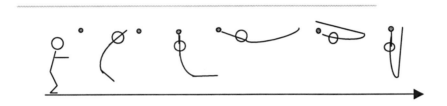

Octagon Glides & Toes To Bar

1. Have your gymnast grasp bar and place their feet on an octagon or barrel. Instruct them to hold a hollow and slightly piked position and to keep their buttocks under while gliding.
2. Once on the bar, your gymnast must swing\glide forward and roll backward, keeping their legs on the barrel\octagon for three full glides. (Your gymnast must reach an extended position each time.)
3. Once your gymnast is extended for the third time, instruct your gymnast quickly to bring their toes\ankles to bar and hold them on the bar, even when the body swings\falls (due to gravity) to the hanging position.

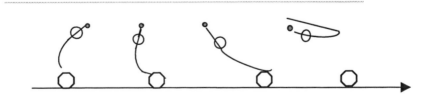

Notes

CONDITIONING AND DRILLS FOR BARS 6

Band Kips

1. Wrap a therapy band or surgical tubing around the base of very sturdy equipment such as the beam, vault, or bar base.
2. Instruct your gymnast to lie on their back and grasp the band or surgical tubing. Their head should be closer to the base than the feet.
3. Have your gymnast bend their knees.
4. Make sure your gymnast is holding the band very tight, while keeping their arms straight and close to their body.
5. Next instruct them to pull the band toward the ceiling and then down toward their thighs.
6. They may then return the band to the starting position slowly using the same direction, toward the ceiling then toward the base.
7. This should simulate the upper body while performing a **kip** on the bars.

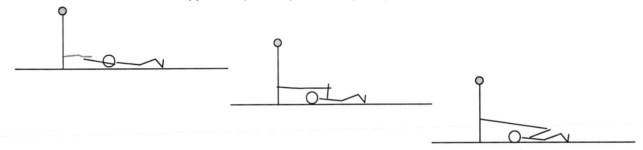

Band Casts

1. Wrap a therapy band or surgical tubing around the base of very sturdy equipment such as the beam, vault, or bar base.
2. Instruct your gymnast to lie on their back and grasp the band or surgical tubing. Their feet should be closer to the base than their head. Bend knees.
3. Have your gymnast bend their knees.
4. Make sure your gymnast is holding the band very tight, while keeping their arms straight and close to their body.
5. Next instruct them to pull the band toward the ceiling and then down toward their ears\head..
6. They may then return the band to the starting position by slowly using the same direction, toward the ceiling then down toward the base\thighs.
7. This should simulate the upper body while performing a **cast to handstand** on the bars.

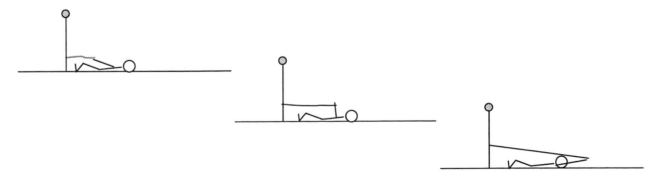

Collected and Presented by Karen M. Goeller Copyright © 2001

Notes

CONDITIONING AND DRILLS FOR BARS 7

P-Bar Walks and Swings

1. Set up either 2 stacks of panel mats or 2 blocks, leaving enough space to walk between.
2. Place a mat on the floor between the mat stacks.
3. Have your gymnast stand between the mat stacks.
4. Next instruct them to support themselves, one hand on each mat stack.
5. While supporting themselves, they must keep their feet off the floor, and may bend their knees if necessary,
6. Once they can support themselves in this position, **allow them to walk** with their hands\upper body supporting them to end of stack\block.
7. Once forward walking is performed, your gymnast should walk backwards.

1. Once walking forward and backward is mastered, have your gymnast remain in the center of the stack supported on their hands with their feet off the floor.
2. Next have them (tap) **swing their lower body** (legs) forward and backward, keeping their arms straight and attempting to swing to a handstand at the top of backward swing.

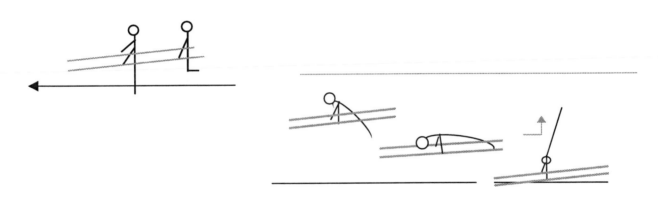

Octagon Rocks

1. Place an octagon\barrel in front of a floor bar.
2. Have your gymnast stand between the bar and octagon\barrel.
3. Instruct them to place their hands on the floor or bar and shins\ankles on the octagon\barrel.
4. While keeping their arms straight, body tight and hollow, and legs on the octagon, instruct them to rock forward and backward.
5. They should rock from their ankles to their knees, keeping from allowing their thighs to touch octagon.
6. Your gymnast should go from a stretched shoulder position to a planche position and then return to stretched shoulder position.

Collected and Presented by Karen M. Goeller Copyright © 2001

Notes

Octagon Rock to Handstand

1. After the Octagon Rock is mastered, have your gymnast perform the octagon rock and hold at the forward\planche position.
2. Once your gymnast can reach the planche position from the octagon rock comfortably, instruct them to lift one leg toward a hansdstand while keeping their shoulders forward.
3. Remind them to keep tight and their shoulders in the correct position to simulate shoulder movements for the cast handstand.

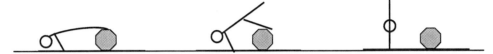

Bounce to Handstand

1. Place either a "Handstand Trainer" or a mini trampoline in front of a floor bar. The lower end should be closer to the bar than the higher end if using a mini trampoline.
2. Have your gymnast place their hands on the floor bar and their shins on the bungee or feet on the trampoline bed.
3. Instruct them to lift one leg, kick it down to jump start the bounce.
4. Once in the air, have them open their shoulders to perform a handstand and then planche to return to the starting position. The goal is to perform several repetitions with a tight& hollow body, and their shoulders forward(planche) when not in the actual handstand.
5. Instruct your gymnast to bounce, lifting and lowering their body as a unit rather than piking and opening at the top.
6. When done correctly, this should simulate a cast handstand.

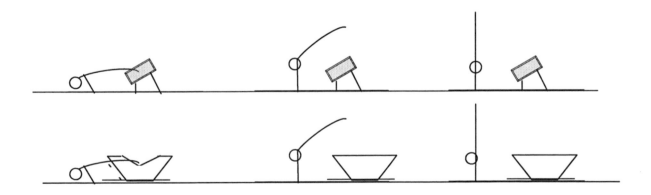

Notes

Presses on Block

1. Use a spotting block, a mat stack, or the beam.
2. Have your gymnast start in front support on block, mat stack, or beam.
3. Instruct them to slightly lean forward and slide their legs up the block. mats, or beam until their ankles reach the top edge of the block, mat, or beam..
4. Once they are as high as they can go instruct them to either press/slide back down to front support and repeat press.
5. Or place their feet on top of block, mats, or beam to a standing or squatting position.
6. Or roll out of press onto block or mats.
7. Or press handstand out of press/slide up.

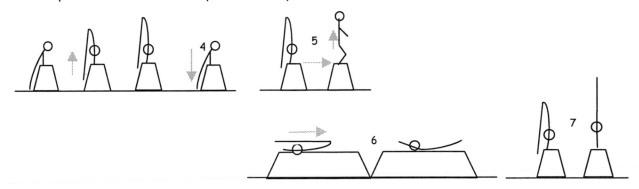

Cast & Hold

1. Be ready to spot.
2. Have your gymnast start in a front support on the bar.
3. Hold your gymnast's shoulders and shins to prevent them from falling.
4. Instruct them to cast: pike and lean forward, look at knees, and then quickly and immediately kick legs back, push hips off bar, and push down on bar with hands and upper body.
5. Gymnast must remain tight and hollow.
6. Hold them in the air\cast position, and help your gymnast rock forward and back as if performing the octagon rock drill, but this time it is on the bar.
7. Once your gymnast is able to remain tight while being held in the correct position as well as while rocking forward and back, you may be able to lift them up to a handstand position.
8. Return your gymnast back to the bar slowly and carrefully in a support position.

Notes

Wall Climbs

1. Have your gymnast stand with their back close to padded wall.
2. Instruct them to place hands on floor\mat approximately 1-2 feet from wall.
3. Next have them place their feet on the wall.
4. Once your gymnast is strong enough in that position...
5. Instruct them to simultaneously walk their hands in towards wall and feet up wall towards ceiling until their forehead touches wall and their shoulders touch their ears.
6. Keeping their arms straight, instruct them to *either* walk back out, remaining very tight.
7. *Or* keeping arms straight, allow them to slide their feet back down the wall and roll out.
8. **Once this is mastered,** have your gymnast perform shoulder shrugs in the handstand position before rolling or walking back out.
9. Take precautions...the mat must be secured against wall and the inexperienced gymnast must be spotted and\or watched closely in order to prevent falling into arched position against wall.

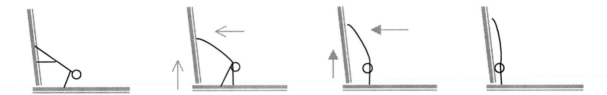

Back Extension to Climb

Once the Wall Climb and Roll Down are mastered.

1. Have your gymnast stand on a mat with their back facing a padded wall, approximately body-distance from the wall, including their arms.
2. Instruct them to perform a straight-arm back extension and aim their feet toward wall.
3. Once their feet reach the wall, instruct them to continue to walk in toward the wall, sliding their feet up the wall simultaneously.

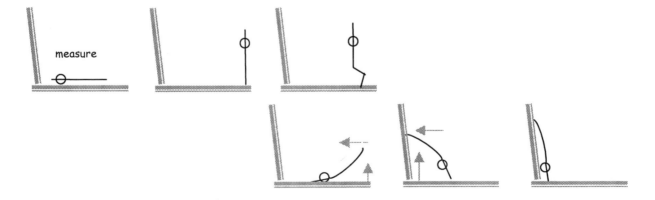

Straight Arm Cast/Lift Drill

1. Be ready to spot.
2. instruct your gymnast sit on the floor with their knees bent and back against a padded wall.
3. Have them hold a straight bar or two light dumbbells with their palms facing the floor.
4. Instruct them ton raise their arms forward and upward simulating a cast to handstand on bars.
5. Once at the top, instruct them to lower the bar or dumbbells by bringing them forward and then to the low front position.
6. Make sure the keep their elbows nearly straight, but not locked on this drill.

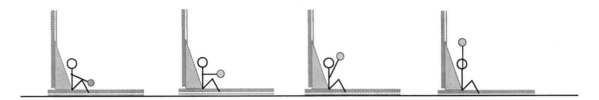

Lie Down Cast/Kip Drill (Very advanced version of Band Kips and band casts)

1. Be ready to spot.
2. Have your gymnast lie on their back between two folded panel mats.
3. Mats must be higher than your gymnast for safety reasons! (If the bar falls, it should land on the mats, not your gymnast.)
4. There should be room for the bar to touch floor after it is lifted over your gymnast's head for full range of motion. (cast handstand)
5. Instruct your gymnast to hold the straight bar (that is long enough to rest on both of the mats).
6. The bar can have weights, depending upon the strength and experience of the gymnast and coach.
7. Start with the bar at thigh level, resting on the mats. (to simulate a front support)
8. Your gymnast may need more spot on the initiation phase of the exercise than the return phase. Be prepared to spot all phases of this exercise.
9. Instruct your gymnast to keep their arms straight, but not to lock their elbows.
10. Next, instruct them to lift the bar up toward ceiling and then toward the floor above their head to simulate a cast to handstand motion with their upper body.
11. Instruct your gymnast to continue to hold the bar securely and then lift bar up toward ceiling again and lower to the mat right above their thighs to simulate a kip with their upper body.

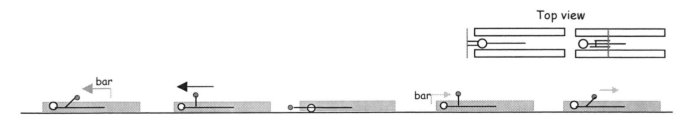

Notes

Clear Hip Body Shape Drill

1. Have your gymnast start in a front support position on the bar.
2. Be ready to spot.
3. Instruct them to perform a small cast.
4. As they pull back towards bar they should drop their shoulders back and down. Their head should stay in. (similar to a "hollow rock' position)
5. Instruct them to remain tight and hollow and help them hold this position upside down with their thighs near\on the bar. (A front support upside down)
6. Lift your gymnast by their shoulder to return them to a front support position.

Block Clear Hip Drill

1. Have your gymnast stand on a block\mat stack holding the low bar.
2. Be ready to spot.
3. Instruct them to jump up and forward to reach a position as if they just performed a cast.
4. Instruct them to immediately fall back, keep their head in and body hollow\tight, and then circle bar.
5. Try not to allow their legs to touch the bar at any time throughout the circle around the bar.
6. When your gymnast can see the floor, instruct them to flick their wrists in order to get their hands on top of bar.
7. Once their hands are on top of the bar, tell them to push down with their arms, and raise their arms towards ears\open up the shpulder angle in order to land on block again.
8. As your gymnast becomes more advanced, you may be able to raise the block or platform they are landing on in order to simulate a higher clear hip.

Notes

CONDITIONING AND DRILLS FOR BARS 13

Tap Drill

1. Have your gymnast hang from the bar.
2. Be ready to spot.
3. Instruct your gymnast to squeeze everything in their body tight.
4. Once they are tight, instruct them to stick their armpits out toward the wall they can see. This will cause them to become just slightly arched. (Their toes should be slightly behind them.)
5. Next instruct them to pull their arm pits back in. They should pass through the straight position to a hollow position. At that point their toes should be slightly front of them.
6. Remind your gymnast to squeeze their buttocks the entire time; this exercise requires movement of the shoulders.
7. Repeat the positions using the shoulders to form the arch and hollow shapes necessary for tap swings, giants, and several other skills on bars.

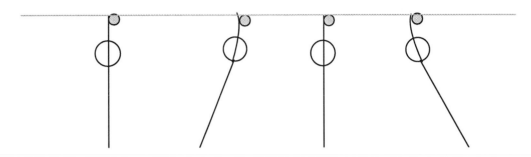

Tap Swing to Candlestick

1. Have your gymnast perform 2-3 tight tap swings.
2. Be ready to spot.
3. At the top of the last swing instruct them to shape their body in a candlestick position.
4. Once shaped like a candlestick, instruct your gymnast to release bar and hold the candlestick in the air.
5. Either **hold your gymnast** in this position in air and slowly lower them to their feet.
6. Or place a **porta/resi pit** or very soft and high stack of mats to allow your gymnast to land on their back on the soft mat stack.

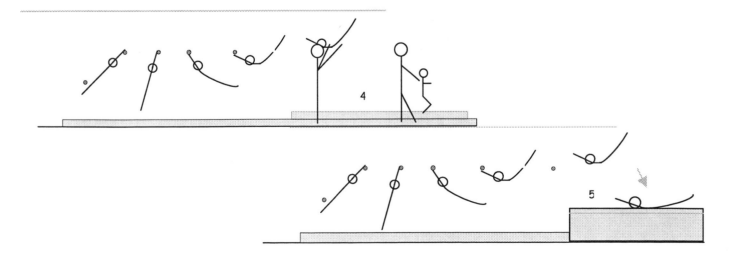

Notes

Butt Swings - (Forward & Backward)

1. Have your athlete start seated on the floor with their knees in a **tucked** position.
2. Instruct them to lift their feet off the floor, keeping the tucked position.
3. Next instruct them to place their hands on the floor beside their body, but reach forward.
4. Once they have reached forward, instruct them to shift their weight from their buttocks to their hands, lifting their buttocks off floor.
5. Once they have shifted their weight, have them swing their buttocks forward, passing their arms with their hips.
6. They should finish the exercise with their hands on the floor in back of their body.
7. Keeping their feet off the floor, your gymnast should repeat the exercise several times, down the vault runway, the floor exercise area, or a long strip of mats.
8. **Once your gymnast masters the exercise forward,** have them perform the same drill in reverse, traveling backwards.
9. **After your gymnast has mastered the tucked** butt swing, have them try it with straight knees, in a pike-V position.

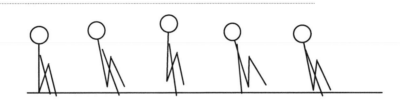

Straddle Butt Swings

1. This is the same drill as the "Butt Swings" above, , but in a straddle position.
2. Make sure your athlete's hands must remain in front them as they travel forward.
3. Once forward is mastered, have your athlete travel backward.
4. When your athlete's buttocks is lifted off the floor, their legs should also leave the floor.
5. Again, have them repeat the exercise down the vault runway, the floor exercise area, or a long strip of mats.

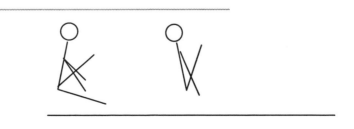

Notes

Scooter Pulls\Pushes

1. Have your gymnast sit on their feet while kneeling on a flat board with wheels. (anything as low to ground as a skateboard)
2. Instruct your gymnast to reach forward placing both of their hands (palms or fingertips) on the floor with their fingers facing direction they are traveling in.
3. Using their arms, have them pull their body\wheeled board forward while their hands appear to be pushing the floor back. This exercise should simulate the end of a glide kip on bars with their arms.
4. Once forward is mastered, have your gymnast perform this drill in reverse, traveling backwards. Backwards should simulate a cast on bars.

Rainbow Pulls\Pushes

1. Have your gymnast get in a long, round, push up position shaped like a rainbow. They should be hollow and not have any shoulder or hip angles. Instruct them to squeeze their buttocks and stay that tight throughout the exercise.
2. Once in the correct position, have your gymnast walk using only their hands\arms and keeping their feet pointed.
3. They will literally drag their feet while each arm simulates the movement of a kip on bars.
4. Once your gymnast has mastered this rainbow Walk, have them perform the exercise moving backwards. When they walk backwards, they should flex their feet.
5. Have your gymnast repeat this exercise down the vault runway, the floor exercise area, or a long strip of mats.

Notes

CONDITIONING AND DRILLS FOR DANCE 1

Hip Flexor Drills - Straddle

1. Have your athlete sit on floor in straddle position.
2. Instruct them to place their hands in front of their body on the floor slightly further than a natural\relaxed placement in order to force the athlete to lean forward.
3. Keeping their legs straight, feet pointed, and buttocks on floor, instruct them to lift both of their legs to shoulder height and then return to starting position.
4. Have your athlete repeat this exercise several times quickly.
5. As your athlete gains strength in their hip flexors, their hands can be placed further from their body.

Hip Flexor - Piked

1. Have your athlete sit on the floor in a pike position. (legs straight out in front and together)
2. Instruct them to place their hands on the floor next to their knees.
3. Keeping their legs straight, feet pointed, and their buttocks on the floor, instruct them to lift both of their legs to shoulder height and then return to the starting position.
4. Repeat several times quickly.
5. As your athlete gains strength in their hip flexors, their hands can be placed further from their body, closer to ankles.

Hip Flexor Drills with Added Lift.

1. Have your athlete sit on the floor in a straddle position.
2. Instruct them to place their hands in front of their body on the floor slightly further than a natural\relaxed placement in order to force the athlete to lean forward.
3. Have them lift one leg to shoulder height.
4. Instruct your athlete to keep that leg up and then lift their other leg to shoulder height.
5. As soon as their second leg is at shoulder height, instruct your athlete to lift both legs even higher. ("1, 2, crank")
6. Make sure your athlete continues to lean forward throughout exercise and keep excellent form.

In fond and loving memory of Renville Duncan, Our Choreographer and so much more...

Both Crank Higher

Notes

CONDITIONING AND DRILLS FOR DANCE 2

Renvillations

1. Have your athlete place the heel of one foot on top of a folded mat. This foot remains on the mat throughout the exercise but it does turn over at one point.
2. Their other leg is behind them as if they are sitting in a split with one foot on a mat and hands supporting them. (over split)
3. Instruct your athlete to lean forward slightly and lift their back leg off the floor.
4. Once their leg is lifted, instruct them to swing the lifted leg to the side, then forward and above the mat. (Avoid cutting the leg through!)
5. At this point, your athlete should have the swinging/circling leg in the air in front of their body and hands supporting their weight behind them. Make sure your athlete's buttocks never touches the floor.
6. Keeping that leg in the air and the other foot on the mat, instruct your athlete to quickly turn their body so that leg in air remains in place, but is now behind and above the body. Athlete's belly is facing floor.
7. Next, have your athlete swing/circle the same leg sideways again, then forward to land in a split with the back foot\shin on the mat. The same foot has been on the mat the entire time.
8. Once this split is reached, instruct your athlete to lift up their body slightly and turn their hips to face the mat in the starting position.
9. The athlete's legs must remain perfectly straight throughout this exercise. Allow them to make the natural adjustments/cuts with their hands as the leg is circled.
10. Constantly remind your athlete to keep perfect form in order for the drill to produce the correct results...a great leap!

In fond and loving memory of Renville Duncan, our choreographer and so much more...

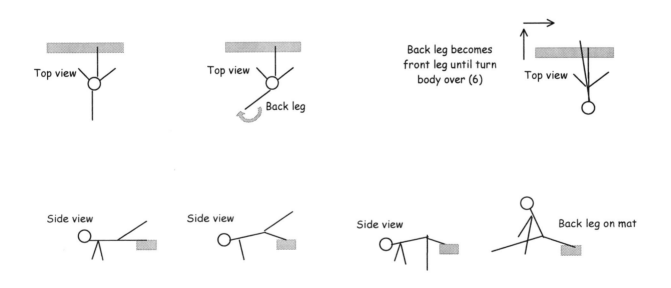

Notes

CONDITIONING AND DRILLS FOR DANCE 3

Lean Back

1. The spotter\coach must be very experienced and strong to spot this drill. It is impossible to do this drill without an extremely good spotter.
2. Place a soft mat behind the athlete in case they become loose and fall.
3. Have your athlete lift their leg so that spotter is holding their ankle.
4. The spotter steps (w\o shoes on) on the athletes foot that remains on the floor in order to prevent the athlete from slipping\falling.
5. The athlete must hold one leg up in front, their head to the bottom foot in one straight line, and their arms side/middle.
6. While the athlete remains extremely tight the spotter holds their ankle and lowers them towards the floor. Athlete's back is facing floor. Athlete is actually leaning back holding a straight body while the spotter is holding one leg.
7. Once the athlete's head comes close to the floor\mat, the spotter raises them back up to the starting position. (standing with one leg in the air)

In fond and loving memory of Renville Duncan, Our Choreographer and so much more...

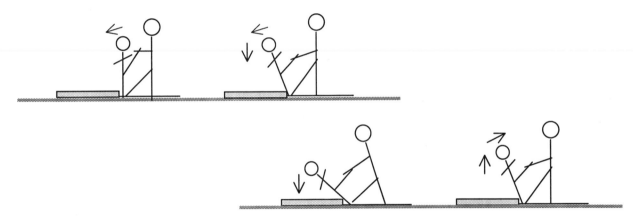

Attitude Leg Lifts

1. Have your athlete sit on the floor with one leg in front of their body, bent at the knee and turned out.
2. Their other leg should be behind their body, bent, and turned out.
3. Their foot should be directly behind opposite hip and their knee should be directly behind the same hip.
4. Instruct your athlete to sit up tall and lift their front leg several times quickly. Make sure they lift their entire leg as a unit, keeping their ankle and knee even in height throughout the exercise.
5. Next, have your athlete sit tall and lift their back leg several times quickly. Their knee and ankle must lift as a uunit, remain at same height throughout the exercise.

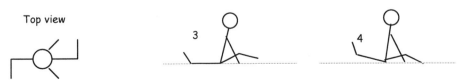

Top view

3

4

Notes

CONDITIONING AND DRILLS FOR DANCE 4

Swing Splits on Bars

1. Have your athlete hang on a bar without any obstacles in path of their legs.
2. Instruct them to lift their legs up to a split quickly. (one leg at hip height in front of body and the other leg at buttocks height behind the body)
3. Be sure to remind them not to allow their legs to wander off to the sides, but to keep their legs in line with their hips.
4. Once your gymnast is in the correct position, instruct them to hold the split for a few seconds.
5. Next allow them to bring their legs back down and together.
6. Once your athlete's legs are together, instruct them to lift their legs quickly again, but working the opposite split.

Switch Leg Drill

1. Have your athlete hang from a bar again.
2. Instruct them to lift their legs up to a split quickly and then switch legs to opposite split position rather than bringing legs down to rest in between splits.
3. Instruct your athlete to remain square (both shoulders and hips same distance from wall they are facing or even with bar) and repeat this exercise several times, but perform one drill at a time.

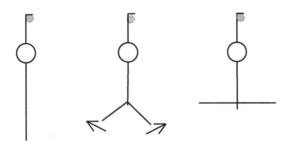

Hanging Hip Flexor Drills - Straddle

1. Have your athlete hang on a low bar without any obstacles in path of legs.
2. Keeping their legs straight, feet pointed, and buttocks under, instruct them to lift both legs so their legs are at hip height. The hanging straddle is the starting position.
3. Next have your athlete lift their legs approximately 6-8 inches higher than hip height and then return to starting position.
4. Have your athlete repeat this exercise several times quickly. These are mini straddle leg lifts.

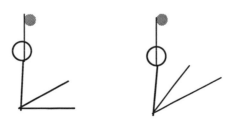

Notes

Notes

CONDITIONING AND DRILLS FOR DANCE 5

Hip Flexor Stretch

1. Have your athlete lie on their back on a mat stack or spotting block.
2. Make sure their buttocks is at the edge.
3. Instruct them to hold one knee close to their chest, with a bent leg.
4. Next instruct them to lift their other leg above their body with their toes pointed toward the ceiling. This leg can be bent\relaxed as well.
5. Have your athlete slowly lower the relaxed leg so that it is hanging below the top level of the block or mat stack.
6. Make sure their hanging leg is lined up with their hip and not off to the side.
7. The hip flexor will be slowly stretched while hanging in this position.
8. Your athlete may wear a light ankle weight, depending upon their level and flexibility.

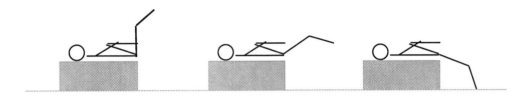

Hip Flexor/Hamstring Stretch

1. Have your athlete kneel on the floor with one leg in front of their body.
2. Instruct them to shift their weight to their front leg, pushing their hips forward.
3. Once their hips are forward, instruct them to lift their back foot, bending at the knee. Make sure they keep their knee on the floor.
4. Make sure their foot is not over their knee for the safest and most efficient stretch.
5. Keeping their feet in place, have your athlete shift their hips back to stretch the front leg's hamstring muscles.
6. Make sure your athlete is not sitting on their back foot, and that the very tops of their thighs are touching each other in order to keep the stretch\ athlete square. Stretching square will help keep your athlete's splits and leaps square.

Notes

Notes

CONDITIONING AND DRILLS FOR DANCE ELEMENTS 6

Partner Standing Stretch & Strength

1. Allow an experienced coach or partner to stretch your athlete's leg by lifting their leg high enough to feel a good stretch in the back of their legs, mostly hamstrings.
2. Make sure your athlete keeps their supporting leg straight and their hips even.
3. And make sure your athlete keeps their supporting foot flat on the floor and both of their legs turned out slightly.
4. The partner is doing the lifting\stretching for your athlete for the first 10-15 seconds.
5. **After the first 10-15 seconds** of being stretched, instruct your athlete **to** resist the partner in the stretch position for another 10-15 seconds.
6. After the resistance phase, the partner continues to stretch your athlete slowly and carefully.
7. Next, have the partner hold the heel of your athlete slightly (1" - 2") lower than the highest stretching point and then instruct your athlete to **lift their leg up** and out of partner's hand several times quickly. (short leg lifts\kicks)
8. Once your athlete is able to lift their leg from the partner's hand, have them **lift again and hold** their leg up for as long as possible. (Most athletes can only hold this very high leg lift position for only a few seconds.)

Split Stretch

1. Have your athlete kneel on the floor with one leg in front of their body. Once in that position, instruct an experienced coach or partner to stand behind your athlete
2. Your athlete should then be instructed to hold the partner's legs.
3. Once both are in position, instruct your athlete to lift one leg forward and up.
4. The partner will then grab hold of your athlete's leg.
5. Once the partner has your athlete's leg and your athlete is holding the partner's legs, the partner will pull your athlete's leg up to stretch them.
6. Instruct the partner to press their knees forward enough so that the athlete does not fall down while being stretched.
7. The supporting leg/knee must remain in one position and their hip on the supporting leg side must remain straight and open.
8. Your athlete's hips must remain square.
9. Have your athlete perform the same resistance and lifting portions as described in the previous stretch after the initial stretching is done.

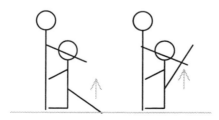

Notes

CONDITIONING AND DRILLS FOR DANCE ELEMENTS 7

Form Drills\Leg Extensions

1. Have your athlete lie on the floor on their stomach.
2. Next have them place their feet on a panel mat or something fairly soft and 8-12 inches high.
3. Instruct another athlete who is close in weight to slowly get in a sitting position on the back of your athlete's knees with their legs crossed and fingertips on the floor for balance.
4. Instruct your athlete to keep their hips and chin on the floor.
5. Once both are in position, instruct your athlete to straighten their knees and hold the straight leg position for about 10-15 seconds.
6. The straight and relaxed movement should be done nonstop until several repetitions are completed.

Leg Curls

1. Have your athlete kneel on the floor with their hips open and their buttocks off their feet.
2. Next have another athlete hold your athlete's ankles to prevent lower leg (shin) from leaving the floor.
3. Instruct your athlete to lower their body as a unit towards the floor., keeping their hands in front of them to contact the floor as if in the push up position.
4. Once your athlete is close to the floor they may use her hands (only slightly) to push the floor, but must use their hamstrings to pull them back up to the starting position.
5. Make sure your athlete's hips remain open throughout the entire exercise…the buttocks never leads the body on the way up.

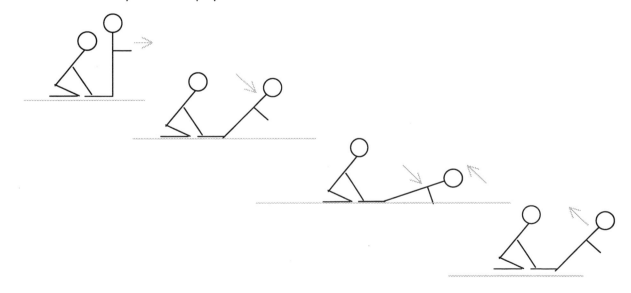

Notes

Kicks (Forward and Back)

1. Have your athlete stand up straight and tall.
2. Instruct them to quickly lift one leg up high in front of their body.
3. Make sure they kick up rather than out.
4. Make sure they keep their legs straight, chest up, back straight, shoulders back, and if on balance beam their hips square.
5. Have your athlete either return to the starting position or step forward to kick the other leg keeping their legs straight, chest up, and hips square if on balance beam.
6. Make sure your athlete performs this exercise kicking forward and traveling forward and have them perform this exercise kicking back while traveling forward.

Kick-Kick Bend (Split Leap Drill)

1. Have your athlete perform the front kick, then lower the same leg\foot and place their weight on that foot.
2. Next instruct them to immediately kick the other leg up behind their body. As they are performing the back kick, instruct them to simultaneously bend the supporting leg as if they are simulating the bent knee\proper landing for a leap. It is important that their knee be in line with their center toe as their knee is bending and straightening rather than leaning inward.
3. Make sure your athlete keeps their shoulders back and if on balance beam, their hips square.

Kick-Switch-Bend (Switch Leap Drill)

1. Have your athlete perform a front kick.
2. Next have them immediately swing the same leg\lifted leg back down and then back to end in a high position behind their body.
3. As their leg is rising behind their body, instruct your athlete to bend the supporting leg to simulate the landing of a switch leg leap.
4. It is important that your athlete's knee be in line with their center toe as their knee is bending and straightening rather than leaning inward.
5. Make sure your athlete keeps their shoulders back and if on balance beam, their hips square.

Notes

Notes

Ankle Drills

1. These drills can be done on balance beam with one foot in front of the other (back foot toes touch front foot heel and both turned out slightly. Toes should remain on top surface of the beam.
2. Or they can be done on the floor with feet in parallel on the floor or facing side on beam and heels below the level of the surface of the beam for a better stretch.
3. Instruct your athlete to keep their chest up, buttocks under, and if on beam to remain square.
4. Have your athlete bend their knees to feel a stretch in their Achilles and ankles.
5. Instruct them to keep their knees bent and lift their heels as high as possible, pushing their feet forward. (forced arch)
6. Keeping their heels high, instruct them to straighten their knees so that they are high on the balls of their feet (releve).
7. Next have them lower their heels to start the exercise again.

Towel Exercises for Arch\Foot Strength

1. Have your athlete stand with their toes and top portion of their feet on a towel or soft cloth.
2. Instruct them to use their toes to pull the towel so that it ends up crunched under their feet.
3. As your athlete is pulling the towel with their feet, their arches usually lift so that the athlete is leaning slightly toward the outer edges of their feet.
4. Once this is mastered, the athlete can place a small object on the towel in order to add a little weight to the exercise.
5. This usually helps prevent the arches of the feet from sagging inward.
6. After performing this exercise for an extended period of time, landings should feel more comfortable and be safer.
7. Once this is mastered, a small weight can be placed on the towel.

Notes

Band Point & Flex (Ankle Strength)

1. Have your athlete sit on the floor with their legs straight out in front of them, a pike position.
2. Instruct them to place an exercise band around the bottom of their feet and hold the ends of the band with their hands.
3. Next instruct them to point their feet as far away as they can.
4. Once they point their feet as much as possible, they must flex their feet by bringing their toes up and toward their body.
5. Have your athlete repeat the point and flex positions using the exercise band as resistance for their feet, ankles, and lower legs.

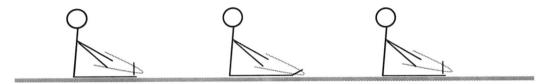

Foot Circles (Ankle Strength)

1. Have your athlete sit at the end of the balance beam or anything narrow with their heels right at the edge.
2. Next tie an exercise band so that it forms a circle\loop.
3. Instruct your athlete to wrap the circle\exercise band around the top of both of their feet. The band is around the feet and the feet are at the edge of a beam.
4. Once in place, instruct your athlete to keep their heels on the beam or narrow table and move their toes outward. Their heels remain in place while their toes make a complete circle outward, down, in, and back up.
5. Have your athlete continue to circle their toes for several repetitions.
6. After outward circles are performed going out first then down, instruct your athlete to have their toes go down, out, then back up for a change.
7. Again, have your athlete perform several repetitions.

Foot Alphabet (Ankle Strength & Stretch)

1. Have your athlete sit with their legs stretched out in front of them. (pike position)
2. Instruct them to draw the letters of the alphabet in the air with their toes.
3. Their feet should be moving in several different directions as they write each letter, therefore thoroughly stretching and strengthening their ankles.

There is no illustration for this exercise.

Notes

CONDITIONING AND DRILLS FOR PRESS HANDSTAND 1

Seal Press (Abdominal & Upper Body Strength)

1. Have your athlete lie on the floor, face/belly down.
2. Next have them place their hands in a pushup position.
3. Instruct them to push up/straighten their arms keeping their hips and legs on the floor. (seal/cobra position)
4. Make sure your athlete keeps their hands in place, legs straight, and feet pointed (top of feet on floor).
5. Instruct them to slide their feet towards their hands using their abdominal and upper body muscles.
6. Their buttocks should lift\rise towards the ceiling.
7. Next either have your athlete walk their hands forward and back out to the starting position, or slide their feet out and back down.
8. Other options are to have your athlete roll out from the top\finish position.
9. If your athlete is a gymnast, you can have them press to a handstand in a tuck, pike, or straddle from the position where their buttocks is at the highest point of the exercise.
10. Instruct your athlete to perform several repetitions or to travel a certain distance such as down

<u>Notes</u>

CONDITIONING AND DRILLS FOR PRESS HANDSTAND 2

Lift Feet, Lift Butt

1. Have your athlete sit on the floor in a straddle position.
2. Instruct them to place their hands on the floor in front of their body.
3. Have them lift their feet and legs off the floor.
4. While keeping their feet and legs off the floor, instruct them to lift their buttocks up.
5. The goal is to try to lift their buttocks higher than their head, which is the first half of a press handstand.
6. Instruct your athlete to repeat several times.

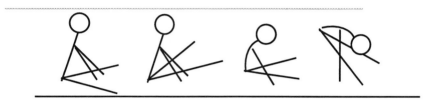

Stalder Roll on Panel

1. Have your athlete sit on a panel mat in a straddle position.
2. Their feet should be resting on the floor on each side before they begin.
3. Instruct them to lift their buttocks off the mat and their feet off the floor as if they are performing the Lift Feet/Lift Butt Drill.
4. Instruct your athlete to press\push down on the mat with their hands, lifting their buttocks.
5. Once their buttocks is high enough, instruct your athlete to roll out on the mat.

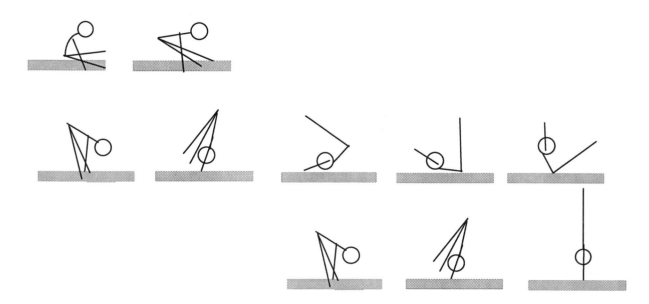

Notes

CONDITIONING AND DRILLS FOR PRESS HANDSTANDS 3

Press Lean

1. Have your athlete stand with their hands flat on the floor in front of their body.
2. Instruct them to position their legs in a straddle.
3. Next have them shift their weight from their feet to their hands. They must then hold their weight on their hands while leaning forward. This will allow them to get comfortable in the pressing position.
4. Make sure your athlete holds this position at least 10 seconds each time.

Press Lean, Lift One Leg

1. Have your athlete perform the "Press Lean." While all of their body weight is on their hands, instruct them to lift one leg about six inches from the floor.
2. Make sure they hold this position for at least 10 seconds before repeating the exercise with their other leg lifted.

Press Lean Lift to Straddle Through

1. Have your athlete perform the "Press Lean." While all their body weight is on their hands, instruct them to lift both of their legs approximately six inches from the floor.
2. Once their feet are off the floor, instruct them to straddle through with their legs to finish in a straddle L position. Instruct your athlete to hold the straddle L position as long as possible.
3. Your athlete can also press back up half way, similar to the Lift Feet/Lift Butt Drill.

HS Press Through

1. Have your athlete kick to a straight handstand.
2. Once in the handstand, instruct them to straddle their legs and tuck their buttocks under.
3. Next, have them slowly lower their legs and bring their legs through and forward to a straddle L position.
4. Once they are in the Straddle L position, instruct your athlete to press back up again, as if performing the Lift Feet/Lift Butt Drill.

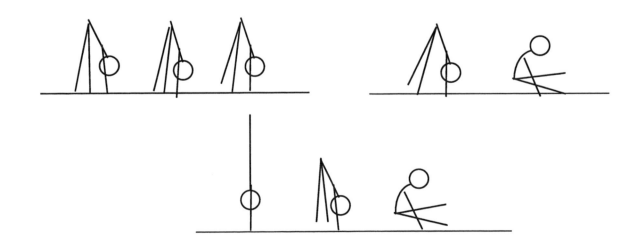

Notes

CONDITIONING AND DRILLS FOR PRESS HANDSTANDS 4

Press Lean Feet on Mat

1. Have your athlete stand with their hands flat on the floor in front of their body. They must be standing in front of a panel mat.
2. Next have them place their feet on a panel mat with their legs in a straddle position.
3. Once in place, instruct your athlete to shift their weight from their feet to their hands.
4. Make sure they hold their weight on their hands getting comfortable in pressing position.
5. Once comfortable, instruct your athlete to lean forward even more and lift their feet from mat.
6. Have them straddle wider in the handstand position and bring their feet together over their body to end in a straight handstand.

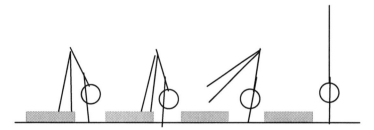

Roll Up Wall

1. Have your athlete straddle in front of a padded wall with their back facing the wall.
2. Once in place, have them perform the Press and Lean Drill placing their back on the wall.
3. Instruct your athlete to press their back against wall.
4. Once your athlete's back is pressing on the wall, have them perform a small roll up the wall and straddle their legs even wider.
5. Once in a straddle handstand, your athlete can bring their feet together to a straight handstand.
6. Instruct your athlete to either step down or reverse the exercise by pressing on the wall as they lower their feet to the starting position.

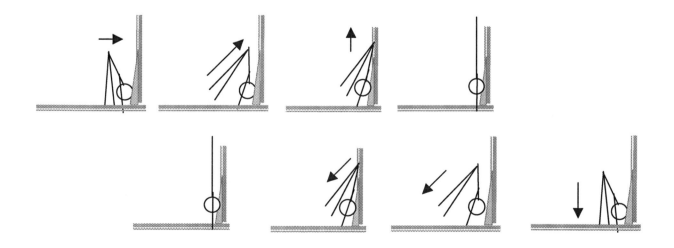

2003 Goeller
You Perform
The Way
You Practice

Item	Price Each	Quantity	Total
Over 75 Drills Book	$16.95		
Over 100 Drills Book	$24.95		
Ankle\Foot Exercises	$13.95		
Cast HS Drills	$13.95		
Press HS Drills	$12.95		
Running Drills	$13.95		
Dance Drills	$22.95		
Back Handspring Drills	$13.95		
Walkover\Limber Drills	$19.95		
100 Drills Book & BHS Pack	$38.90		
100 Drills Book, BHS, WO	$58.85		
100 Drills, Cast, Press, BHS	$65.80		
All 7 Drills Packs	$97.79 ($108.65 - 10%)		
(Cast, Press, Run, Dance, BHS, WO, Ankle)			
100 & All 7 Packs	$120.24 ($133.60 - 10-%)		
FAQ's Book	$14.95		
100 Drills & FAQ's Book	$39.90		
100, FAQ, & All 7	$133.70 ($148.55 - 10%)		
		Sub-Total	
		Shipping	
	Total enclosed or to be applied to credit card		

MasterCard
VISA

www.gymcoach.net

Shipping Calculations

Cost of items	Inside USA	Outside USA
$0.01 - $24.99	$4.75	$15.00
$25.00 - $39.99	$6.50	$18.00
$40.00 - $64.99	$8.75	$22.00
$65.00 - $134.99	$10.00	$26.00
$135.00 - $159.99	$15.00	$30.00
$160.00 +	Call for shipping quote	

Call for Brochure Today!
888-496-8749
www.GymnasticsDrills.com

For fastest service, order through our website, www.gymcoach.net.
Other ordering options…
Send a check payable to: Advertising Works 32 Algerine Street, Berkley, MA 02779
Call 888-496-8749 or Fax form to: 775-582-7916

Name _____ Club Name _____ :

Billing Address _____ :

Shipping Address _____ :

Billing Phone _____ Alt Phone _____ :

Charge Card Number _____ :

Type of Charge Card _____ Exp Date _____ Security Code (on back) _____ :

Signature _____ :

The purpose of the separate drills packs is for those coaches who would like to post the drills on the wall. The drills in the Run, Press, and Dance pack are in the drills book. There are more Cast Handstand drills in the 100 drills book than there are in the laminated Cast Handstand pack. The Back Handspring drills are not in either drills book. With the exception of a few stretching drills, the drills in the Walkover Pack are not in either drills book With the exception of two drills, the Ankle exercises are not in the drills books.

www.gymcoach.net   info@gymcoach.net

NOTES

Printed in the United States
128376LV00001B/50/A